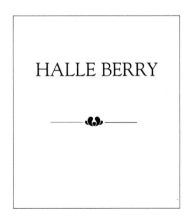

HALLE BERRY

HALLE BERRY

Corinne J. Naden and Rose Blue

CHELSEA HOUSE PUBLISHERS
Philadelphia

Chelsea House Publishers

Editor in Chief	Sally Cheney
Associate Editor in Chief	Kim Shinners
Production Manager	Pamela Loos
Art Director	Sara Davis
Director of Photography	Judy L. Hasday
Cover Designer	Keith Trego

The Chelsea House World Wide Web address is
http://www.chelseahouse.com

Produced by Pre-Press Company, Inc.,
East Bridgewater, Mass.

3 5 7 9 8 6 4

Library of Congress Cataloging-in-Publication Data

Naden, Corinne J.
    Halle Berry / Corinne J. Naden and Rose Blue.
        p. cm. — (Black Americans of achievement)
    Includes bibliographical references and index.
    Summary: A biography of the actress who won a Golden Globe Award in 2000 for her leading role in the
television movie "Introducing Dorothy Dandridge."
    ISBN 0-7910-5802-6 (alk. paper) — ISBN 0-7910-5803-4 (pbk. : alk. paper)

    1. Berry, Halle. 2. Motion picture actors and actresses—United States—Biography—Juvenile literature.
3. African American motion picture actors and actresses—United States—Biography—Juvenile literature.
[1. Berry, Halle. 2. Actors and actresses. 3. Racially mixed people—Biography. 4. Women—Biography.]
I. Blue, Rose. II. Title. III. Series.

PN2287.B4377 N33 2001
791.43'028'092—dc21
[B]   2001037138

CONTENTS

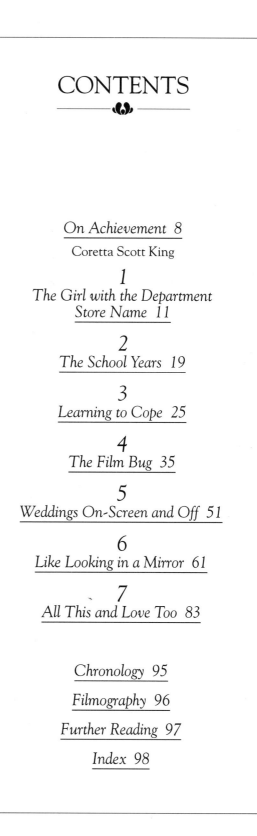

BLACK AMERICANS OF ACHIEVEMENT

MUHAMMAD ALI
heavyweight champion

MAYA ANGELOU
author

LOUIS ARMSTRONG
musician

JOSEPHINE BAKER
entertainer

TYRA BANKS
model

BENJAMIN BANNEKER
scientist and mathematician

COUNT BASIE
bandleader and composer

ANGELA BASSETT
actress

HALLE BERRY
actress

MARY McLEOD BETHUNE
educator

GEORGE WASHINGTON
CARVER
botanist

JOHNNIE COCHRAN
lawyer

BILL COSBY
entertainer

MILES DAVIS
musician

FREDERICK DOUGLASS
abolitionist editor

CHARLES DREW
physician

PAUL LAURENCE DUNBAR
poet

DUKE ELLINGTON
bandleader and composer

RALPH ELLISON
author

JULIUS ERVING
basketball great

JAMES FARMER
civil-rights leader

LOUIS FARRAKHAN
political activist

ELLA FITZGERALD
singer

ARETHA FRANKLIN
entertainer

MORGAN FREEMAN
actor

MARCUS GARVEY
black nationalist leader

WHOOPI GOLDBERG
entertainer

DANNY GLOVER
actor

CUBA GOODING JR.
actor

ALEX HALEY
author

PRINCE HALL
social reformer

JIMI HENDRIX
musician

MATTHEW HENSON
explorer

GREGORY HINES
performer

BILLIE HOLIDAY
singer

LENA HORNE
entertainer

WHITNEY HOUSTON
singer and actress

LANGSTON HUGHES
poet

JANET JACKSON
musician

JESSE JACKSON
civil-rights leader and politician

MICHAEL JACKSON
entertainer

SAMUEL L. JACKSON
actor

T. D. JAKES
religious leader

MAE JEMISON
astronaut

MAGIC JOHNSON
basketball great

SCOTT JOPLIN
composer

BARBARA JORDAN
politician

MICHAEL JORDAN
basketball great

CORETTA SCOTT KING
civil-rights leader

MARTIN LUTHER KING, JR.
civil-rights leader

QUEEN LATIFAH
singer/actress

LEWIS LATIMER
scientist

SPIKE LEE
filmmaker

CARL LEWIS
champion athlete

MALCOLM X
militant black leader

BOB MARLEY
musician

THURGOOD MARSHALL
Supreme Court justice

TERRY MCMILLAN
author

RONALD MCNAIR
astronaut

TONI MORRISON
author

ELIJAH MUHAMMAD
religious leader

EDDIE MURPHY
entertainer

JESSE OWENS
champion athlete

CHARLIE PARKER
musician

ROSA PARKS
civil-rights leader

COLIN POWELL
military leader

DELLA REESE
entertainer

PAUL ROBESON
singer and actor

JACKIE ROBINSON
baseball great

CHRIS ROCK
comedian and actor

DIANA ROSS
entertainer

AL SHARPTON
minister and activist

WILL SMITH
actor

WESLEY SNIPES
actor

CLARENCE THOMAS
Supreme Court justice

SOJOURNER TRUTH
antislavery activist

HARRIET TUBMAN
antislavery activist

NAT TURNER
slave revolt leader

TINA TURNER
entertainer

ALICE WALKER
author

MADAM C. J. WALKER
entrepreneur

BOOKER T. WASHINGTON
educator

DENZEL WASHINGTON
actor

J. C. WATTS
politician

VANESSA WILLIAMS
singer and actress

VENUS WILLIAMS
tennis star

OPRAH WINFREY
entertainer

TIGER WOODS
golf star

ON
ACHIEVEMENT

———— ❧ ————

Coretta Scott King

Before you begin this book, I hope you will ask yourself what the word *excellence* means to you. I think it's a question we should all ask, and keep asking as we grow older and change. Because the truest answer to it should never change. When you think of excellence, perhaps you think of success at work; or of becoming wealthy; or meeting the right person, getting married, and having a good family life.

Those goals are worth striving for, but there is a better way to look at excellence. As Martin Luther King Jr. said in one of his last sermons, "I want you to be first in love. I want you to be first in moral excellence. I want you to be first in generosity. If you want to be important, wonderful. If you want to be great, wonderful. But recognize that he who is greatest among you shall be your servant."

My husband knew that the true meaning of achievement is service. When I met him, in 1952, he was already ordained as a Baptist minister and was working toward a doctoral degree at Boston University. I was studying at the New England Conservatory and dreamed of accomplishments in music. We married a year later, and after I graduated the following year we moved to Montgomery, Alabama. We didn't know it then, but our notions of achievement were about to undergo a dramatic change.

You may have read or heard about what happened next. What began with the boycott of a local bus line grew into a national crusade, and by the time he was assassinated in 1968 my husband had fashioned a black movement powerful enough to shatter forever the practice of racial segregation. What you may not have read about is where he learned to resist injustice without compromising his religious beliefs.

He adopted a strategy of nonviolence from a man of a different race, who lived in a different country and even practiced a different religion. The man was Mahatma Gandhi, the great leader of India, who devoted his life to serving humanity in the spirit of love and nonviolence. It was in these principles that Martin discovered his method for social reform. More than anything else, those two principles were the key to his achievements.

These books are about African Americans who served society through the excellence of their achievements. They form part of the rich history of black men and women in America—a history of stunning accomplishments in every field of human endeavor, from literature and art to science, industry, education, diplomacy, athletics, jurisprudence, even polar exploration.

Not all of the people in this history had the same ideals, but I think you will find that all of them had something in common. Like Martin Luther King Jr., they all decided to become "drum majors" and serve humanity. In that principle—whether it was expressed in books, inventions, or song—they found a goal and a guide outside themselves that showed them a way to serve others instead of living only for themselves.

Reading the stories of these courageous men and women not only helps us discover the principles that we will use to guide our own lives; it also teaches us about our black heritage and about America itself. It is crucial for us to know the heroes and heroines of our history and to realize that the price we paid in our struggle for equality in America was dear. But we must also understand that we have gotten as far as we have partly because America's democratic system and ideals made it possible.

We are still struggling with racism and prejudice. But the great men and women in this series are a tribute to the spirit of the country in which they have flourished. And that makes their stories special and worth knowing.

1

THE GIRL WITH THE DEPARTMENT STORE NAME

———— ✿ ————

Oₙ JANUARY 23, 2000, the Hollywood Foreign Press Association presented the annual Golden Globe Awards, a glamorous event, attended by most leaders in the entertainment industry, honoring excellence in film and television. Often, as the Golden Globes go, so go the Academy Awards. That makes the Golden Globes a high-profile ceremony with a huge television audience. Sometimes exposure here can be a big step in a performer's career. On this night the award for best actress in a mini-series or TV movie went to Halle Berry for her leading role in *Introducing Dorothy Dandridge*.

As the audience watched the young star's emotional acceptance, few knew what struggles she had overcome to make it to that stage. But for this night, and perhaps for good, her many struggles—the problems she faced as part of an interracial family plagued by alcoholism and physical abuse, unhappy and sometimes abusive personal relationships, a failed marriage, and the day-to-day coping with a serious illness—were behind her. This was Halle Berry's big night. The Golden Globes marked the first major tribute by her peers for the girl with the department store name.

It is thus difficult to realize that when Halle Berry's parents married in the 1960s, they would have

Halle Berry kisses the Golden Globe she received for her work in the title role of the TV movie Introducing Dorothy Dandridge.

broken the law had they lived in Delaware, Arkansas, Tennessee, Florida, or any of 12 other states. A Supreme Court decision of 1967 made interracial marriage legal, but it didn't make it acceptable in the eyes of many or erase the underlying bigotry. Whether in Birmingham, Alabama, or Cleveland, Ohio, interracial couples generally had a hard time in the 1960s and, in many cases, continue to have problems today.

Halle's parents, Judith Hawkins and Jerome Berry, met in a psychiatric hospital in Cleveland in the 1960s. She was a nurse; he was an aide. Their relationship, on the surface, seemed to be ordinary. They liked each other, began to date, fell in love, got married. But their love story had one big complication: She was white; he was black. In the 1960s it was unacceptable almost everywhere in the United States, for a black person to marry a white person. Before 1967, it wasn't even legal in many states, and interracial couples were thrown in jail for getting married.

That happened to Mildred Jetter, a black woman, and Richard Loving, a white man. After getting married in Washington, D.C., where interracial marriages were legal in 1958, they moved to Virginia, where such marriages were against the law. In 1959, the Lovings were given a sentence of one year in jail. The decision was appealed, and the case made its slow progress through the higher court system, reaching the Virginia Supreme Court in the mid-1960s. The court upheld the conviction, stating that interracial marriage was indeed a felony. The case continued on to the U.S. Supreme Court, where in 1967 the sentence was overturned by a unanimous vote.

In 1966 Judith and Jerome Berry had a daughter, whom they named Heide. Two years later, on August 14, 1968, Halle was born. Berry was named for Halle—rhymes with Sally—Brothers in Cleveland, Ohio, a department store where her mother enjoyed

shopping. The Berry girls spent their early years in a troubled household, where discrimination and prejudice came from many sources.

Besides outright prejudice from strangers, interracial couples often had to endure hostility from their own family. Berry's parents certainly did. Her mother was disowned by her family when she married, and

Halle grew up in a suburb of Cleveland, Ohio, and was named after a large department store in the city where her mother often shopped.

her father's family was afraid that the marriage would not work, that their son would be subject to all kinds of abuse and prejudice, even bodily harm, from people who would not want an interracial couple living next door or eating at the next table. Both families also worried about children. Would they grow up without knowing "who they were"—white or black? They wouldn't belong or fit in anywhere, and no race or ethnic group would really accept them. Halle Berry will tell you that such problems were very real.

Not fitting in is a common complaint of many people of mixed racial backgrounds, including some well-known entertainment personalities who have spoken or written of their sometimes difficult childhoods. Superstar golfer Tiger Woods calls himself Cablinasian, a term that reflects his Caucasian, black, Indian, and Asian roots; singer Mariah Carey is black, white, and Venezuelan; movie star Keanu Reeves is white, Asian, and Hawaiian; television newscaster Ann Curry is white and Asian. Even if their childhoods were sometimes difficult, it is perhaps an encouraging sign of the times that all of these people have managed to lead successful lives.

Although people of different races do marry and have marriages that are strong and healthy and provide good environments in which to raise children, they are still not the norm, and things don't always work out the way they should. The marriage didn't work out in the Berry family. Certainly, the interracial situation was at the root of the trouble. It was perhaps the reason that Halle grew into a shy child who often did not want to leave the house. Her mother often had to coax her just to take a trip downtown. But Halle usually resisted, feeling safer in her own home with her mother and sister, where no one would look at her strangely or make disturbing remarks about her mixed skin color. "The other kids would call me 'zebra,'" she later said. She also recalls having Oreo cookies—black-on-the-outside, white-on-the-inside—placed in her mailbox. Young Halle thus had a lot to contend with during her early years. Lighter skinned than her sister, she had more trouble adjusting to, and being accepted by, the black community in which she lived. And being beautiful, in this instance, only made people envy her.

Besides prejudice to strain the Berry household, there were perhaps even bigger problems. Jerome Berry was an alcoholic who physically abused his wife. When Halle was four years old, he walked out of the house and was gone. No father, no father's income. But at least the threat of physical harm disappeared along with him.

Most people find themselves asking two questions about domestic violence: How can a husband and father physically abuse his wife and children? If violence occurs, why does the wife and/or mother continue to stay in the home?

From the early part of the 20th century, domestic violence was generally something that one didn't talk about. It was embarrassing. Police might thus be called to a home where neighbors had observed a man beating his wife only to be told by the woman that nothing had happened. Also, in many states police were not allowed to arrest a suspected batterer unless a third party had witnessed the beating. Apparently, the victim's accusations and wounds were not considered enough evidence.

Besides the fear of embarrassment, women often stay in an abusive home because there is nowhere else to go. In those families where the man has taken charge of the money, how can a woman pack up the children and flee with no money or ways to care for them? And perhaps the oldest, saddest reason that many women stay in a violent situation is because they just cannot believe that it is happening. When the abusive husband pleads and says it will never happen again, the wife wants desperately to believe this is the truth. But, of course, it generally is not.

In the 1970s, the feminist movement in the United States began to fight spousal abuse in earnest. They fought it by bringing it out in the open and by pushing for federal legislation. It has been a long, hard pull. Thousands of women are still victims today, but the atmosphere is changing.

A major breakthrough in the 1990s was that domestic violence increasingly became regarded as a serious crime. Since 1994, it is a federal crime to cross state lines with the intent to harm a spouse or other intimate partner. A batterer can be sentenced to 10 years in prison for crossing the state line for that purpose, 20 years if inflicted injuries are life threatening, and life in prison if the attack results in the victim's death.

Changes have also occurred in police training in how to respond to domestic violence situations. More and more, law enforcement agencies are adopting a policy of "probable-cause" arrest. If the police are called to a home on a domestic violence case, the suspected batterer is taken into custody even if the wife or another victim does not want to press charges. Oftentimes, a restraining order is issued against a batterer. That means he is ordered to stay a certain physical distance away from the victim at all times. If he violates that boundary, he can be sent to jail. Sometimes the batterer is fitted with an electronic device that informs the authorities of his whereabouts at all times.

Unfortunately, sometimes even such laws and devices don't work. Every year women are harmed or even killed by batterers, even those with restraining orders against them. Many people feel that the only way to deal with this horrendous crime is to educate people in different ways of handling stress and anger, and to provide help to battered victims who want to get away from a potentially threatening situation. Today, there are many organizations, such as the Abused Women's Aid in Crisis (AWAIC), whose first aim is to get women (or men if that is the case) and children out of an abusive situation immediately, before the violence erupts into killing. Their second aim is to provide safe havens for those who have left abusive homes.

Halle's mother was clearly a victim of domestic violence, what has come to be known as the "quiet crime"—rarely talked about, or even known about perhaps, outside of the family. Although attitudes about domestic violence are slowly changing today, Judith Berry and other victims were mainly without help in the 1960s. Halle's mother was pretty much on her own. Besides concern for her personal safety, she had two small daughters to protect.

Although Jerome Berry's physical violence was not directed against his daughters, the threat was always there in such a household. Heide and Halle Berry were not too young to realize what was happening, even if they could not understand it. Living in such a home left scars that would remain all through their lives. At the very least, Jerome Berry gave his daughters a very poor role model by which to judge all men. And by being brought up in a violent home, the girls were placed in danger of becoming the next generation of victims. And this is to some extent what was to happen with Halle Berry. As a grown woman, she endured at least one violent relationship before she realized what it was doing to her and walked out.

In an attempt to protect her girls from the devastating scars of violence, Halle's mother moved her small family to Bedford Hills, a suburb of Cleveland with a population of about 17,000. She worked as a nurse to raise her daughters and provide them with a new beginning.

2

THE SCHOOL YEARS

A SHY AND often troubled Halle Berry began her school years in the Bedford school system. Merry Anne Hilty, a language arts teacher, talked about young Halle Berry in an interview. "She was very quiet," Hilty recalls, "and not a super student. Although she had to struggle for good grades, she did try hard and so was able to maintain a B or C level." Hilty thought that the young girl's shyness stemmed from the absence of her father. "She seemed to need another adult," Hilty said, "to pick up the slack."

> But she and her mother were very close, and Halle's mother was very supportive. She was supportive to both girls. Heide was older, darker complected, and a better student. But the sisters were very close. In fact, the mother and two daughters formed a very close, supportive group, probably to make up for the absence of the father.

Throughout her school years, Berry turned to her teachers for comfort. She got a good deal of that from her fifth-grade teacher, Yvonne Nichols Sims. Later, when Berry went to Bedford High School, Sims became a guidance counselor there. "When Halle moved from Cleveland to the suburbs, there was a definite adjustment period," she says. "Actually, she did not have many problems with her peers in fifth grade. She got along well with the other kids. The community of Bedford was and is integrated. Of

Today Halle's beauty is recognized by Hollywood producers and legions of fans, but her interracial background and fair features made fitting in difficult during her childhood.

19

course, she had the usual preteen problems to deal with—just growing up things—and I tried to help her with those."

Halle remembers her fifth-grade teacher very well and still admires her. In fact, Sims remains a friend of the Berry family. Halle credits her, especially in high school, with "helping me find my way," with making her school years more interesting. To present students with relevant challenges, Sims formed an after-school club dealing with African-American history. She took her group, which included Halle Berry, on field trips to museums, art galleries, and events that emphasized black history and accomplishments. Sims especially remembers their trip to see an exhibit of local artists. "It was Halle's first visit to an art museum," she recalls. "A local artist named Curlee Holden had a collection of paintings concerning the Cleveland school busing issue." After the Civil Rights Acts of 1964, which banned discrimination in U.S. public schools and elsewhere, school busing became a hot topic.

That trip and those paintings "opened Halle's eyes," Sims recalls. "Seeing the accomplishments of African Americans, of African American artists. Dealing with race issues and achievements filled sensitive youngsters such as Halle with a sense of pride and satisfaction." Sims felt that it was important for black youngsters to delve into their roots. She especially felt that Halle needed to have a greater understanding of her African-American half. For a shy youngster like Halle Berry, it was important for her to see that other black Americans had overcome great obstacles in order to achieve their goals.

Perhaps because of the care and attention from her mother and from teachers such as Sims, Halle had grown more confident and popular by the time she reached high school. And perhaps because Bedford High was largely white, she felt compelled

During the 1960s, cities such as Cleveland began busing to desegregate public schools. Learning about that era made a deep impression on Halle.

to succeed to show the other students that she was just as smart as they were. She still worked hard for grades, but she also became a cheerleader, an editor on the school newspaper, and a member of the honor society. And as she grew on the inside, she was becoming more beautiful on the outside as well.

Halle still had to face problems, however. As pretty and popular as she was, she could go only so far before the "race issue" would crop up in some way. Says Sims, "Halle's main challenge at Bedford High concerned the envy of other students because of her charisma, beauty, charm, and the ability to mesh with others."

When it was time to elect a homecoming queen, Halle's looks and popularity ensured that she would be easily nominated. But a number of the students at Bedford High did not take kindly to voting for a black girl. In spite of such opposition, Halle won. In retaliation, some of the students challenged the election, saying that Halle's backers had stuffed the ballot boxes. "That's when the race thing really hit me," Halle says today. "They liked me until I was representing a symbol of beauty in our school."

An investigation had to be conducted. The process was embarrassing and hurtful for Halle, but she refused to give in. Finally, the assistant principal conducted his own investigation and resolved the issue. Halle was the legitimate winner. An old prejudice had been broken at Bedford High, and the school had its first black homecoming queen. Yet, as Halle recalls, the whole episode greatly diminished the joy of her election. However, says Sims, "Halle is very strong. Enduring what she went through in that experience strengthened her and made her better able to face the challenges of adulthood."

It was indeed a challenge for young Halle Berry. Troubled still by the memories of abuse from her father and the breakup of her parents' marriage, she was also still coping with her shyness and the prejudice that never quite seemed behind her. Berry faced the end of her high school years with uncertain thoughts about a career. What would she do now?

3

LEARNING TO COPE

WHILE STILL IN HIGH SCHOOL, one of Halle's friends quietly entered her name in the Miss Teen Ohio beauty pageant. Berry was surprised to find out what he had done, but she was even more surprised when she eventually won the title in 1986. This success was soon followed by others: second place in the Miss USA pageant and third place in the Miss World competition.

Halle's entrance into the pageant world and her modest success was short-lived, however. Just on looks alone, it would seem that Halle Berry could have been very successful if she had stayed on the circuit. However, she decided on another path. She enrolled in Cuyahoga Community College in Cleveland, a two-year school offering, among its many fields of study, courses in communications. Halle decided to enter the field of broadcast journalism.

Halle soon discovered that she had made the wrong choice. Although she did an internship at a local radio station while going to college, it was soon obvious to her that she had no real enthusiasm for the field. So, she left the radio station and dropped out of school. Using the connections she had made during her short pageant stint, Halle headed for Chicago with an eye on a modeling career. New York City might have been more lucrative, but at five foot six, Halle knew she was considered too short for the elite and competitive runways of the

By 1999, when this photo was taken, Halle had already established herself as an actress in movies and on television. But it was while in high school that Halle's physical beauty first became a key component in determining her future. Her beauty opened doors into the worlds of modeling and acting.

Halle (second from left) placed second in the Miss USA pageant and third in the Miss World competition.

Big Apple. Plus Chicago is an easy three-hour drive from Cleveland.

At first it seemed that she'd made another wrong choice. Jobs were hard to come by in Chicago. Eventually, however, she got some ad work modeling lingerie. She also decided to audition for an acting role in *Angels '88,* an update of Aaron Spelling's smash 1970s TV series *Charlie's Angels.* Although Halle didn't get a part, and the show never made it to television, Spelling was impressed with her screen test and urged her to keep trying for an acting career.

The audition encouraged Berry to think about acting. She said later that in the back of her mind, she had always wanted to be an actress. "I remember imitating scenes from the Wizard of Oz," she said. "In fact, I even had the right dog!"

Halle's mother was very supportive of her daughter during some of these early rough spots. She offered this advice: "Keep your chin up. Go do it. But even if you fail, home is always here."

In 1989, a friend from Halle's pageant circuit days gave Halle's name to a New York talent manager, who requested a videotape. He was impressed enough to agree to represent her—on the condition that she agree to give up modeling in Chicago and move to New York City. After much deliberation, Halle decided to make the move.

For a while it looked like this was going to be another bad choice. Nothing happened in New York. With no money coming in, Halle slept in a homeless shelter and later at the YWCA. Then at last it happened—an acting job on a new TV sitcom called *Living Dolls.* The program featured a group of aspiring show-biz young women in the big city. Halle got the part of the brainy but beautiful model in the crowd. If the show caught on, it would give her nationwide exposure. Instead, Halle had to confront a new problem in her life.

Memories of reenacting scenes from the Wizard of Oz helped Halle realize that she had always wanted to be an actress.

One day during rehearsal in 1989, the entire cast and production crew of *Living Dolls* was more than mildly surprised when Halle suddenly collapsed. When she came to, Halle was just as surprised as anyone else. So she went to a doctor, who ordered tests. The result was a scary diagnosis—diabetes.

"In my mind, all I heard was that I'd have to take shots every day and that I could lose my eyesight or my legs. I was scared to death," Halle said later. So, she went to another doctor. The test results were the same—diabetes.

Just what is diabetes? Why was Halle Berry so frightened? In order to be healthy, all the cells of your body need a constant supply of sugar, in the form of glucose. Sugar is the most important source of energy for all living tissue. You get glucose from the foods you eat, mainly carbohydrates such as bread and cereals. After you digest the food, the carbohydrates are converted into glucose. This glucose gets into the cells where it is needed with the help of insulin, a hormone produced by the pancreas.

But what happens if a body doesn't produce enough insulin for this process? What happens if a body doesn't use the insulin properly? In either case, the cells don't get the glucose they need. Unused sugar builds up in the blood. The result is diabetes.

So what? What happens if you have too much sugar in your blood? Your kidneys try to get rid of it through urine. If glucose levels get too high, the kidneys are overworked and don't function properly. Starving the body's cells of glucose can lead to all sorts of problems, such as loss of eyesight or limbs. Diabetes is the leading cause of blindness in people between the ages of 20 and 74. It's also the culprit in about 40 percent of all new kidney disease cases in the United States. In addition, people who have diabetes are as much as four times more likely to have heart disease or a stroke. But even though the disease sounds very frightening, and it is very serious, with care and the right information, a person with diabetes can lead a fairly normal life.

More than 15 million Americans—nearly 6 percent of the population—have diabetes. Health officials think that as many as 5 million people don't even know they have it. Diabetes is a lifelong illness, for which there is as yet no cure. But many people are working to find one and to raise public awareness. Actress Mary Tyler Moore, for instance, who has diabetes, has long been a spokesperson for the American Diabetes Association. Founded in 1940, the ADA is the country's leading nonprofit health organization. Its aim is to prevent and cure diabetes by conducting research and providing information through its programs in all 50 states.

Although we don't know what causes diabetes, we do know that it is inherited. If someone in a family has it, it's likely that down the line, other family members will have it as well. We know that diabetes often occurs in older people and that Hispanics, Asians, Native Americans, and African Americans are at higher risk than the rest of the population. But we don't know why.

There are two major types of diabetes: Type I and Type II. Type I is insulin-dependent diabetes mellitus, or IDDM, which accounts for 5 to 10 percent of all cases. Because this usually strikes people before they are 30 years old, it was once called juvenile diabetes. Type I diabetics produce very little insulin, or none at all. In either case, they require daily insulin injections to stay alive. In the near future, some diabetes patients will be able to take their daily insulin requirements through a nose spray.

Type II diabetes, or non-insulin-dependent diabetes mellitus (NIDDM), is the most common form, accounting for 90 to 95 percent of all cases. People most at risk for this type are those over age 45, those with a family history of the illness, those who are overweight and who do not exercise regularly, and those belonging to certain racial groups. The disease can be mild, moderate, or severe. Some Type II diabetics may be able to control the disease simply by eating a balanced diet and avoiding too much weight gain. Pills are also available for Type II patients. In general, Type II diabetes is not considered as serious as Type I. However, a person with this illness must monitor his or her daily blood glucose levels to avoid serious consequences.

The American Diabetes Association thinks that celebrities such as Halle Berry who have diabetes can be a big help in getting people to pay attention to symptoms and get treatment. Nicole Johnson of Virginia agrees. She was Miss America in 1999, and she has Type I diabetes, diagnosed when she was 19 years old. Like Halle, Johnson thought her world had fallen apart when she heard the news.

Johnson had been entering state beauty contests since her senior year in high school. During one competition, she began to feel kind of shaky and strange. When the feeling didn't go away, she went to an emergency room. The diagnosis was diabetes.

Like Halle, Johnson was shocked and felt that diabetes would take control of her life. She began to live in fear of what her blood glucose monitor would tell her each day. She was constantly afraid each time she had to test herself. In short, the disease was controlling her.

Two years before she entered the Miss America contest, Johnson began wearing an insulin pump, a device that automatically tests blood sugar level and administers insulin accordingly. The pump made a big difference in her control of the disease and her mental outlook. She was able to graduate from the University of South Florida and then from Regent University of Virginia with a master's degree in journalism. When Johnson decided to enter the Miss America contest, her friends told her to forget it, that no one with a medical condition would ever win the title—certainly not someone with an insulin pump beneath her ball gown!

At first Johnson was discouraged by the words of her friends; then she became angry. So, the next year she entered and won the Miss Virginia pageant—insulin pump and all. She was on her way to Atlantic City and the big pageant. Her eventual victory there was a great triumph.

During her year as Miss America, Johnson traveled about 20,000 miles a month with about one day off. She spoke before schoolchildren, at fundraisers, and at political gatherings. Her message was always the same—diabetes is a serious and potentially deadly disease, but it can be treated and you can live with it. Now on the board of the American Diabetes Association, Johnson works to spread the word, especially among children, about staying healthy.

Halle Berry, who has Type II diabetes, became very depressed after she learned the diagnosis—not an unusual reaction, especially in a younger person. Many diabetics are faced with a feeling of helplessness and hopelessness, a sense that diabetes is ruining their life. Fortunately, there are many counseling and support groups, as well as education and medical care organizations, that can show people how to stand up and take back control of their lives.

For some reason, women generally seem to have a harder time adjusting to life with diabetes than men do. In some cases, especially for women who have families, they may feel that they should be taking care of everyone else, not the other way around. Women tend to feel that diabetes makes them different, setting them apart from the family or society. With this comes a sense of powerlessness.

Of course, being different was not new to Halle Berry. She had felt it all her life, growing up in a biracial family, in a home abandoned by her father. In a way, the shyness of her early years returned with the news of the diabetes. She withdrew into herself and simply denied that she had the illness.

Halle eventually began to come out of her shell and face the facts. She has learned to control her illness through alternative medicine, diet, and exercise. Although she takes oral medication, she does not take insulin injections. She volunteers for the American Diabetes Association, helping youngsters who must deal with a serious illness.

4
THE FILM BUG

Halle in the 1995 motion picture Losing Isaiah, *in which she portrays a reformed crack addict fighting to regain custody of the child she had earlier abandoned.*

BESIDES LEARNING TO cope with diabetes, Halle Berry was now out of work. *Living Dolls* had a short TV life and was soon cancelled. "Here I was an ex-model, a former beauty queen, and when *Living Dolls* was cancelled, I was still playing a model," Halle said. "I had the feeling people weren't taking me very seriously."

But Halle vowed to change that. She was certain that acting was the career for her, so she left New York for Los Angeles. It was a good move. She soon won a recurring part on the long-running prime-time soap opera *Knots Landing.* The role wasn't big, but it was work and it was a start.

Her first real movie break came in 1991 with Spike Lee's *Jungle Fever.* Starring Wesley Snipes and Annabella Sciorra, the movie features an interracial romance. For her role as Vivian, a crack addict, Halle, protected by an undercover cop, visited a Washington, D.C., crack house. She said she didn't shower for 10 days to get the feeling of the scene and the character she would play. The tour through the crack house—especially the sight of automatic weapons and knives everywhere and the horror of seeing young girls caught up in this situation—was an eye-opener for the girl from Cleveland.

Director Spike Lee gave Halle's acting career a major boost when he cast her in the role of a crack addict in his 1991 film Jungle Fever.

The movie got generally favorable reviews, and Halle's well-received performance did lead to work in other films. She felt she was taking the first solid steps to a serious acting career.

In 1991, Halle won a small but important part in *The Last Boy Scout,* starring Bruce Willis and written by Shane Black of *Lethal Weapon* fame. In this hard-core action film, Willis plays a fired Secret Service agent, who with an old friend investigates evil doings in the football world. To prepare for her role as a stripper, Halle once again sought out real-life experience to bring to the part. Even before reporting to the set to begin rehearsals, she visited strip clubs and even gave exotic dancing a try at a live performance. Although the film got mixed reviews, *New York*

Publicity shot for Strictly Business. *Many of Halle's early roles relied more on her looks than on her talents as an actress.*

Times film critic Vincent Canby praised Halle: "The best thing in the film is Halle Berry. She is an actress who is going places."

Also in 1991 Halle got a small part in *Strictly Business,* a film about the antics of an up-and-coming businessman and his yuppie girlfriend. Playing a glamour girl, she did not have to go too far beyond her mirror to prepare for the role.

The following year Halle got a more substantial role as Angela, Eddie Murphy's love interest in *Boomerang.* In reviewing the movie, Judy Gerstel of the *Detroit Free Press* called Halle "versatile" and said that her role of Angela was played to "doe-eyed perfection." *Ebony* magazine said she was a "down to earth, drop dead gorgeous woman,"

Halle's part as Natalie in the 1991 Warner Brothers romantic comedy Strictly Business *was not large, but it did give her additional "big screen" exposure. She is seen here with two of her costars, Tommy Davidson (left) and Joseph C. Phillips (center).*

adding that "Berry exudes confidence, having already shattered the Hollywood adage that models can't act."

Such reviews showed that people were beginning to watch Halle Berry. That same year she was named one of the world's most beautiful people by *Us* and *People* magazines.

While still shooting *Boomerang,* Halle heard about a role she truly wanted—that of Alex Haley's paternal and biracial grandmother in a six-hour TV miniseries entitled *Queen,* to be shown in 1993. Back in 1977, Haley had mesmerized a nationwide television audience with *Roots,* the epic story of his ancestors in Africa—from their capture through a life of slavery in America.

Haley had spent 12 years tracing his family roots back to Gambia. Night after night for a week, in

With Eddie Murphy in Boomerang.

white suburbs and inner-city ghettos, Americans were caught up in the saga of one man's family and events that occurred some 200 years before. About 80 million people watched each night's episode as *Roots* became probably the most popular program in television history.

Halle Berry had been one of the 80 million viewers of *Roots* and wanted to be a part of the continuation of the *Roots* saga that was to emerge in *Queen*. "Being from an interracial background myself," she explained, "I felt if I had lived back then, some of those things could have happened to me. I read the script the night I learned Alex Haley was dead, and I couldn't put it down. I knew I had to play this part."

The series producers weren't so sure, thinking that Halle was far too young and too beautiful. But Halle was nothing if not persistent, and after a second audition, she won the role. Besides Halle, the miniseries carried some rather well known and

In 1993 Halle starred in Queen, *an adaptation of a book written by Alex Haley (seen here). But the TV miniseries garnered little of the acclaim bestowed on the earlier* Roots.

respected names—Danny Glover, Ruby Dee, Ossie Davis, Ann-Margret, and Martin Sheen.

Presented in three parts, the story opens in Alabama in 1841, two decades before the Civil War. The first segment focuses on Queen's parents. James Jackson Jr., heir to the Forks of Cypress plantation, has an affair with Easter, a beautiful black woman on the plantation, whom he loves but cannot marry. They have an interracial child named Queen, who looks white. She grows to adulthood as the Civil War begins and swears she will never leave the plantation on which she grew up and that she will make the white family love her.

In part two, Queen does remain on the battered and wasted plantation after the war. At last realizing that her white family will never love her, she leaves

to find a new beginning, which she does as a white woman. She becomes engaged to a southern gentleman, who leaves her when he discovers the truth. Eventually, Queen meets a proud black man with whom she has a child. Because of his commitment to organizing black workers, he is hunted down and lynched.

Queen becomes a maid on a plantation and eventually marries a widower with a small farm. But plagued by years of terror and unhappiness, Queen suffers a mental breakdown and spends time in an institution. When she is released, she looks forward to some time of happiness with her husband.

A grandly staged production, *Queen* was, nonetheless, coolly received by the critics. The *Washington Post* called it "criminally slow and riddled with

Halle in Alex Haley's Queen. *Halle identified with the biracial heroine and said of her role, "I felt if I had lived back then, some of those things could have happened to me."*

Halle as the slithery Miss Stone distracts a befuddled Fred in The Flintstones.

showboat melodrama." *New York Times* critic John J. O'Connor was a bit more kind to Halle, saying that she maintained a "steady flow of lovely persuasion." Others, however, thought she was not quite up to carrying the important central role of such a marathon story.

Following her role in *Queen*, Halle appeared in two mostly forgettable movies. The first was *The Program* (1993) with James Caan, in which she plays a coed in a story that examines the problems of college football players and abuses by big-time college football programs. This movie was more notable because of scenes that were cut after one teenager was killed and others were injured while imitating portions of the movie. Next came *The Flintstones*, with Halle playing the role of Miss Stone, a glamorous type who distracts poor Fred Flintstone by slithering across his desk.

In *Solomon and Sheba*, a 1995 cable television movie, Halle was cast as the legendary queen of

Sheba and Jimmy Smits, of TV's *NYPD Blue,* was the king of Israel. It served as a showpiece for Black History Month that year.

After finishing her role as a long-ago queen, Halle went back to being a crack addict—on screen, that is. In *Losing Isaiah,* she plays a crack-addicted woman who tosses her infant son into the trash. The infant is adopted by a white social worker (Jessica Lange). The film traces the attempt by Halle's character to straighten out her life and reclaim her son. The reviews were mixed. Some were favorable, but *Films in Review* said, "Berry is in over her head." However, it did comment on her good looks.

Once again, Halle Berry's almost startling beauty seemed to be getting in her way. This would not be the first or the last time that Hollywood—and perhaps the real world for that matter—would look into a pretty face and see nothing behind it.

At times emotionally wrenching, Losing Isaiah *struck a chord with critics and moviegoers alike.*

Losing Isaiah gave Halle the opportunity to work with one of Hollywood's most respected actresses, Jessica Lange, who portrayed a social worker in the film.

Sometimes it hurts to be beautiful: Hollywood has a long history of seldom looking beyond a pretty face. Three Hollywood legends epitomized a beauty that often obscured underlying talents.

Mararita Carmen Cansino (1918–1987) became the beautiful red-haired Rita Hayworth, sex symbol of the 1940s' silver screen. Her looks were so adored that during World War II, her pinup picture in *Life* magazine was reproduced in millions of copies that were sent to U.S. servicemen overseas. When an atomic bomb was dropped on Bikini, an atoll in the Pacific Ocean used as a U.S. test site, Hayworth's picture was painted on it. Although she starred in a number of films, most notably *Gilda* (1946), the critics almost never got past her beauty to concentrate on her dancing or acting talents.

Norma Jean Mortenson became Marilyn Monroe (1926–1962), a sex goddess whose face and figure were legendary. Usually cast as a dumb blond, she eventually astounded critics with her subtle performance as a saloon singer in *Bus Stop* (1956). She also proved to be a memorable comic actress in *Some Like It Hot* (1959), a film in which Jack Lemmon and Tony Curtis play two musicians trying to avoid the mob by joining an all-girl band.

Elizabeth Taylor first had to "put up" with beauty in *National Velvet* (1944) when, at the age of 12, she played a girl who enters her horse in the famed Grand National Steeplechase. When she grew up, Taylor was regularly declared to be the world's most beautiful woman. More scrutinized for her eight off-screen marriages than for her acting ability, Taylor won her first Oscar for *Butterfield 8* (1960), in which she did not give her best performance.

Halle Berry hopes that Hollywood will start to look below the surface in the 21st century, and she wants to be part of making this happen. But it hasn't been easy thus far, and her first film of 1996 didn't help. In *Executive Decision,* with Kurt Russell, Halle plays a flight attendant. Janet Maslin of the *New York Times* called her performance "window dressing." Things began to look up, however, later in the year with the release of *The Rich Man's Wife.* It didn't get four stars, but Halle, who plays a blackmail victim and murder suspect, got some favorable reviews.

In another 1996 film, *Race the Sun,* Halle is cast as a peppy, idealistic teacher opposite James Belushi as a gruff shop teacher. The setting is Hawaii, where Halle's character prods her underachieving, racially mixed high schoolers into believing that they can design and build a solar-

In Race the Sun *Halle plays Sandra Beecher, a teacher who tries to inspire her racially mixed class of underachievers.*

powered car. With Belushi's character grudgingly in tow, they win a local race, which allows them to compete in a 2000-mile contest in Australia. Though perhaps a bit improbable, the film had a feel-good, funky quality.

Halle's next movie was a 1997 comedy called B*A*P*S (which translates as Black American Princesses). She plays one of two black waitresses in Georgia—the other is played by Natalie Desselle—who set out for Los Angeles with dreams of making big money by setting up a combination beauty salon and restaurant. Rather improbably, they wind up living in the mansion of a wealthy old white man played by Martin Landau. Landau becomes so enchanted by these two women that he starts eating soul food and spouting rap. The intended humor, however, was lost on most every critic, although some did think that Halle was funny.

Her next film, in 1998, was *Why Do Fools Fall in Love?* This film tells the story of the ill-fated 1950s teenage rock 'n' roller Frankie Lymon, played by Larenz Tate. Lymon died of an overdose at the age of 26 and left behind three wives. Halle played one of them—Zola Taylor, lead singer of the Platters. The three women he supposedly married—apparently he was a bigamist as well—vie for his royalties after his death. Critics felt that the best parts of the movie were when Little Richard appeared as himself, although there was also some praise for scenes involving Halle and the other two women, played by Vivica A. Fox and Lela Rochon. In general, however, the critics didn't much like the film.

Halle knows that most would-be film stars quickly learn that they may have to suffer through some bad times and some bad productions. After the television movie *The Wedding* (discussed in the

Bulworth was well received by both critics and audiences alike and gave Halle a chance to prove her talents.

next chapter), Halle finally got a part in a well-reviewed film called *Bulworth* (1998), which starred and was directed by Warren Beatty. In this political satire, Beatty plays a burned-out California senator running for election in 1996. Halle plays a would-be assassin named Nina, a leftist who gives the senator a lesson or two about politics. Reflecting on his past voting record and other actions, the senator's conscience finally catches up to him. To make up for his past performances, he decides to tell the truth at all times and to embrace the black community. The film satirizes the political process in America and has many biting comments on the problems of poor people.

Throughout the 1990s, Halle kept looking for better and better roles in which she would not be totally defined by her racial background or even her beauty. Sometimes she was successful, sometimes not. In the meantime, there was another side to Halle Berry that her fans knew little about—a side that involved love and marriage. Oddly enough, the wedding that took place in Halle's personal life was followed by a wedding in her film life as well.

5

WEDDINGS ON-SCREEN AND OFF

Halle and her husband, major league baseball player David Justice. The two were married on New Year's Day 1993.

E VER SINCE HIGH SCHOOL, Halle Berry had been serious about making it in the entertainment field. That left little time for a personal life, except for occasional dates. Even those, she later admitted, had not been very successful. When she and Wesley Snipes were filming *Jungle Fever,* they became an item in the gossip columns. The romance didn't last, and Halle was very upset for a time. Things got worse after that, however. She began dating a man she will not name but refers to as "someone well known in Hollywood." The relationship became abusive, to the point that he struck her and punctured her left eardrum, causing her to lose 80 percent of her hearing in that ear.

Halle seemed to be following the pattern of children of an abusive parent when they themselves pick an abusive romantic partner. Mental health professionals feel that this often happens because the child has no positive opposite-sex role models. A daughter who has lived with an abusive father may find it difficult to understand what makes up a healthy relationship with another man. Abuse, to her, may be the norm. Without realizing it and because of her background, she may seek out a potentially abusive romantic partner because that is what she is used to.

In addition, she may lack self-esteem, feeling that somehow the abuse was her fault. In other words, she is getting what she deserves.

Halle, of course, had the double problem in her background of abuse and alcoholism. The children of an alcoholic parent, or parents, also often have serious problems in adulthood. Some become alcoholics themselves. Psychiatrists say that children of alcoholic parents may have trouble coping with their own success. No matter how high they rise or how well they do, they continue to lack self-worth. And it is difficult for them to form healthy personal relationships.

All these problems are compounded when, as in Halle Berry's case, the father abandons the family. He may not have been a good husband or father, as in the Berry household, but nonetheless his departure created a void that left long-lasting scars. Once again, the child feels to blame and there is a sense of rejection that is especially hard to deal with in later life.

However, despite her background, Halle insisted that her one abusive incident was the last. She left the relationship immediately and has had no similar problems since. However, she has been criticized by some colleagues for not revealing the name of the man who struck her. They believe that she should not be protecting him and that other women should be warned. Halle remains silent.

Halle's next relationship started out as a fairy tale but ended in turmoil. Some critics might even say that the turmoil was borderline abuse. In February 1992, she was in Charleston, South Carolina, shooting the HBO miniseries *Queen*. One day she attended an MTV celebrity baseball game and saw Atlanta Braves outfielder David Justice. Recalls Halle, "I had cardiac arrest. He was so gorgeous."

Sometime later, Halle was interviewed by a reporter from Cincinnati, Ohio, Justice's hometown.

*Throughout their marriage,
David Justice and Halle
Berry spent much time
apart—the inevitable result of
their chosen careers.*

The reporter, who knew that Justice was a Halle Berry fan, requested a signed photograph to give to the ballplayer. Halle not only signed her name but added her telephone number. She recalls that their first phone conversation lasted for hours.

Soon a picture began taking shape in her mind of David Christopher Justice, born in 1966. At Covington Latin High School in Kentucky, he played basketball and soccer and ran track and field. After some time in the minor leagues, he joined the

Halle, as Josie Potenza, in A Rich Man's Wife appears to have it all until her husband is murdered and she becomes the chief suspect. Meanwhile her own marriage to David Justice was suffering from the strain of two highly stressful careers.

Atlanta Braves in 1989. In 1990, he was named National League Rookie of the Year. In 1997, Justice was traded to the Cleveland Indians.

It wasn't long after their first phone conversation that Justice showed up at the ballpark with Halle's name tattooed on his arm. Then, on January 1, 1993, they were married in his Atlanta home. The columnists began speaking of another Marilyn Monroe/ Joe DiMaggio romance, another marriage between a Hollywood beauty queen and a well-known baseball slugger.

Berry's marriage lasted longer than did the nine-month Monroe/DiMaggio union—Halle and Justice were divorced in 1996—but the trouble began long before the end. First and foremost was the problem of balancing two professional careers as well as households in both Atlanta and Los Angeles. Their lives were not simple. As a professional baseball player, Justice had to spend a good deal of the seven-month season—including playoffs and World Series—on the road. As an actress, Halle might be working in Los Angeles or any location around the country or the world. For instance, in 1995 Justice hit a sixth-inning home run in Atlanta to help win game six of the World Series for the Braves. Halle would have loved to have been there to see it. Instead, she was in Seattle, shooting *The Rich Man's Wife*. "But what could I do?" she asks. "Could I say, 'By the way, can I have this week off? My husband is in the World Series.'"

There were other problems, too. She claimed that Justice did not understand her career and was jealous of her on-screen relationships. He claimed she was suspicious and threw tantrums. Obviously, there was trouble in paradise. Perhaps the final blow came when Justice was picked up by Florida police for being in an area known for drugs and prostitution.

As trouble in the marriage continued to deepen, Halle says that it reached a low point when Justice came to her home and threatened to break the windows if she did not let him in. She called the police and that ended the incident. She says of that time and that experience, "I married Dave because I fell in love, or what I thought was love. I know my dad's abuse definitely screwed me up. I didn't know how to pick a mate.... When I had to call the police and seek protection from a man I loved so much—that I still love—I thought 'this is rock bottom.'" She adds, "I think once you really love someone, a little piece of you always will...."

A few months later, the marriage was over. The hurt of it still haunts her. She had always thought marriage would be for life and so the idea that Justice really wanted a divorce was very hard for her to accept. She says, "I do keep telling myself that this is one of life's lessons, and as long as I can learn something from it, then all the pain will be worth it."

Two years after her divorce, on February 23, 1998, Berry was involved in another wedding, this one strictly on film. ABC aired Oprah Winfrey's production of a two-part TV miniseries entitled *The Wedding*. It was based on an expansive novel by Dorothy West, one of the last surviving members of the famed Harlem Renaissance, a period of artistic life and creativity that took place in the 1920s in Harlem. Set in the early 1950s, the story focuses on an impending interracial marriage between a beautiful, well-to-do black woman and a poor white musician. It deals with racial pride and the strength of commitment just days before the wedding in this upscale black community on the resort island of Martha's Vineyard, Massachusetts.

For Halle, the opportunity to work with Oprah Winfrey was too good to pass up. Oprah was well established as one of the most influential black women in the entertainment world. At the time that *The Wedding* went into production, Oprah had appeared in many films, including *The Color Purple*, which was based on Alice Walker's Pulitzer Prize–winning book. Oprah had received an Academy Award nomination for her performance. She was the first black woman, and only the third woman in history, to own her own production studio, Harpo Studios. She was seen on television daily as the host of a syndicated talk show, and was well known for supporting projects that championed black culture, history, and artists. Her production studio was already working that same year on bringing to theaters the film version of Toni Morrison's Pulitzer Prize–winning book, *Beloved*, starring Winfrey and Danny Glover, and now Oprah wanted Halle to be involved in one of her projects. Here was an opportunity for Halle not only to work with one of the most powerful women in both film and television, but also

Entertainment icon Oprah Winfrey enlisted Halle for a starring role in her production of The Wedding.

to break free from some of the stereotypes of her previous roles.

Halle, who to this point had played strippers, junkies, and fluffy sex symbols, settled into the role of debutante Shelby Coles, who is the youngest daughter in a wealthy and respected family, five generations strong. Just prior to her wedding to a poor white musician, Mende Howell (played by Eric Thal), Shelby is torn by the attentions of a well-to-do black man, Lute McNeil (played by Carl Lumbly), who does not want her marriage to take place. In the end, Shelby Coles makes the decision to marry the man she loves . . . who presumably is the white musician, but the ending leaves the viewer in at least a little doubt.

The Wedding clearly dealt with a subject Halle well understands: interracial love and marriage. The entire range of emotions is portrayed—family reaction, bitterness, and standing up against generations of family prejudices, attitudes about mixing of the races, and bigotry, as well as addressing the question whirling in the minds of many biracial children: Who am I really? Halle says that people frequently have told her that she is just as much of one race as another, just as much white as black. But in reality, she says that's not true. "When I walk out in the world, I'm seen as a black woman. That's the reality."

Following the release of *The Wedding,* Halle appeared on *Good Morning America.* Chantal Westerman, interviewing her, talked about the TV movie and expressed surprise at the levels of prejudice, such as the issue of Shelby Coles's sister in the film marrying a man whose skin is darker than her own.

Halle replied, "Most white people don't realize that within the black race, there is our own prejudice that we suffer from because some people still believe that if you're lighter, you're better. I know I dealt with that growing up, of darker-skinned black people thinking, 'Oh, well, what do you know about being discriminated against. You're high yellow, your mother's white, you don't know.'" Halle is able to see all sides of the situation. "What they don't know is that to white America, I'm very black. And I'm discriminated against the same way they are. Because to a lot of white people, black is black. They don't care what shade you are, you're black, you're not white."

Reflecting again on her recovery from her divorce, that dark period in her life, she said:

> There'd never been another time in my life when I thought that I would not survive it. I've always been a survivor. Knowing that I did, I think, is what you see today, the confidence to live through something that seemed like it was going to kill me, to wake up on a morning when I thought I had no reason to live, and to still be here. That's what you're seeing, the sense of self and the security and the confidence to know that if I survived that, you know, come on, life. . . . I'm equipped.

That's the new Halle Berry—a person learning to cope.

6

LIKE LOOKING IN A MIRROR

Halle, seen here in the role of Dorothy Dandridge, *found many parallels between her life and that of the ill-fated actress, from the 1950s and 1960s.*

IN 1995 AUDIENCES flocked to theaters to see a film about a group of middle-class women dealing with the daily struggles of their relationships, careers, and lives. The film, *Waiting to Exhale,* grossed over $72 million and surprised many of Hollywood's top producers with its appeal to both blacks and whites. The majority of the cast, the director, and the producers of *Waiting to Exhale* were African American.

Even with the great strides that black actors and actresses have made in the film industry, it is still considered an oddity for a "black" film to do well in Hollywood. Discrimination still exists, as Halle had noticed often through her years struggling to establish herself in Hollywood. Clearly, however, black directors, producers, and actors have made progress in breaking through the barriers. This became even clearer to Halle as she was presented a project that opened her eyes to the determination of black actresses who had come before her.

In 1998, HBO began production of a made-for-television movie that would tell the story of Dorothy Dandridge. Dandridge was a black actress who fought against discrimination in Hollywood and asked that she be judged by her on-screen talents, not the color of her skin. Many actresses worked along with Dandridge to open doors that would have otherwise been closed to Halle.

One of the first black actresses to make a name for herself in Hollywood was Hattie McDaniel. McDaniel began her career as a performer while travelling with vaudeville acts and minstrel shows all across the country. With the help of her brother, she found work on a popular radio show in Los Angeles and was soon noticed by film producers. In 1932 she made her first appearance in film when she sang a duet with Roy Rogers in *Judge Priest*. McDaniel soon began to work in other films, appearing with Shirley Temple in *The Little Colonel* and, in her most famous performance, playing Mammy in *Gone with the Wind*. *Gone with the Wind* helped create new opportunities for African Americans in Hollywood. McDaniel's outstanding performance in the film earned her an Academy Award for best supporting actress in 1939, the first time a black had won an Oscar.

Lena Horne was another actress who stood up to the racial divides in Hollywood. Starting her career as a dancer in Harlem's Cotton Club, Horne was noticed by Broadway producers and soon appeared in a number of all-black performances. She soon left New York and travelled as a singer before being signed to a seven-year contract with MGM Studios. Her signing with MGM was a significant milestone in Hollywood: it was the first time an African American was signed to a long-term contract with a major studio. Even with the guaranteed work, however, Horne found that Hollywood wasn't ready to promote a black star. Most of her film roles involved her performing only a short set, either singing or dancing. When appearing in films with white cast members, she seldom received any speaking roles. It was only in all-black films, such as *Cabin in the Sky*, that Horne found roles that truly displayed her talents as an actress.

Yet, it was the life and career of Dorothy Dandridge that touched Halle Berry the most. When

Hattie McDaniel, who won the Best Supporting Actress Oscar for her role as Mammy in Gone with the Wind, *helped open doors for other black actors.*

Halle took on the job of portraying Dorothy Dandridge—the tragic film goddess of the 1950s, who was Hollywood's first African-American movie star and the first black woman to be nominated for the best actress Oscar—it was a bit like looking in a mirror. Like Halle, Dandridge was glamorous, beautiful, and biracial. Dandridge was born in City Hospital in Cleveland, Ohio, as was Halle. Both women suffered through the problems of a fatherless home, failed marriages, and failed relationships.

Ultimately, Dorothy Dandridge found that the struggle to overcome the prevailing prejudices around her was simply too great a strain. In the Hollywood of the 1950s, a black actress—no matter how light-skinned, no matter how beautiful or talented— did not receive a lot of film offers. As a biracial

Lena Horne was the first black actor to sign a long-term contract with a major film studio. Still, she often received only small roles that involved either singing or dancing.

This photo of Dorothy Dandridge accompanied a news release about her death, dated September 18, 1965. The caption read, "the cause of death was the infection that was spread through her system as the result of marrow poisoning resulting from a broken toe." The true cause of death was a drug overdose.

woman, Dandridge struggled to find acceptance among blacks and whites. Her life, marred by unhappiness, ended tragically and prematurely when she died of an overdose of antidepressant drugs at the age of 42.

Halle Berry no doubt lives in a better, more enlightened, more tolerant world, but she says that she still must face the same career problems. Even so, she is determined that any similarities between her and Dandridge will go only so far, that she will learn to be wiser, stronger, and more in control of her career.

When Dorothy Jean Dandridge was growing up, her friends called her "angel face." A beautiful child,

Ruby Dandridge (shown here) left her husband, Cyril, and raised her two daughters, Vivian and Dorothy, on her own.

she got a lot of attention. Years later, a childhood friend recalled that every once in a while, she gave Dorothy a smack just because adults were always talking about how beautiful she was.

Dorothy's parents, Ruby Butler and Cyril Dandridge, met and married in Cleveland, Ohio, in 1919. Both were of mixed racial background. Ruby was a strong-willed, restless woman who would later pursue an acting career of her own. Cyril, a draftsman, was the only child of a modestly well-off family.

In 1921, Ruby and Cyril had their first child, a daughter named Vivian. Cyril was blissfully content with family life, but Ruby was bored. So when Vivian was two months old, Ruby packed her belongings and walked out. Cyril found her and persuaded her to return. On November 9, 1922, their second daughter, Dorothy Jean, was born. Five months later, Ruby felt trapped once again. She packed her belongings and, with the two girls, walked out again. This time she didn't go back.

Through all their growing-up years, the Dandridge girls never saw their father. In fact, Dandridge's mother told her daughters that their father was dead. Later, she admitted he was alive but said he had deserted them. Actually, Cyril Dandridge tried to persuade his wife to return with the children, but she would not. He filed for divorce in 1924—a rare occurrence for a black man at the time—and sought custody of the girls. He lost, although he kept up the fight until the divorce was granted in 1933. Nevertheless, in young Dorothy's mind, he had abandoned them.

Interested in a movie career for herself, Ruby Dandridge sang or recited poetry at local church and social groups. She soon realized, however, that Dorothy was a great crowd pleaser and encouraged her as well as Vivian to perform.

Dorothy grew into a dreamy, shy young woman with dark magnetic eyes, Caucasian features, and golden-colored skin. A friend described her as "absolutely gorgeous." Her mother was often somewhere pursuing a career, leaving the sisters in the care of a stern woman friend whom they called Auntie Ma-Ma. Dorothy quickly discovered that she was happiest when performing, that for her the world of fantasy was much less threatening than the real world.

After the stock market crash in 1929, Ruby remained bent on pursuing a movie career and moved the family, along with Auntie Ma-Ma, first to Chicago and then to Los Angeles. They moved into a house so small that in later years Dorothy would

Hattie McDaniel shows off her Oscar. In the race-conscious climate of the time, McDaniel hadn't even been allowed to attend the premiere of Gone with the Wind *in Atlanta.*

suffer breathing problems whenever she was confined in too small a dressing room. But at least the girls, who had been tutored at home, got to go to school for the first time, Dorothy at the age of eight. Vivian progressed quickly, but Dorothy's education had not been so thorough and she never did learn to read well.

In 1934, the "Dandridge Sisters"—Vivian, Dorothy, and friend Etta Jones—won an amateur radio contest for their singing. They were the only blacks in the running. A black casting director, Charles Butler, recommended them for a bit part in a musical called *The Big Broadcast of 1936*, which starred the great entertainer Bill "Bojangles" Robinson, the master tap dancer. This is the first record of Dorothy Dandridge, barely 13 years old, on film. Her film career had begun.

The Dandridge Sisters got other jobs after that, which kept them out of school from time to time. But

Ruby pressed on, assuming the role of pushy stage mother. Interestingly, she never seemed to acknowledge any discrimination or prejudice in Hollywood, although Dorothy did. For instance, in 1939, when black actress Hattie McDaniel won the Oscar for best supporting actress for her role in *Gone with the Wind*, she was not invited to the premiere of the film in Atlanta. The movie studio was afraid that southerners would be upset if a black woman appeared at the glittering festivities. From then on, Dorothy Dandridge never had any illusions about race barriers in Hollywood, although she did persist in believing that things could be changed.

In 1938, Ruby got a booking for the girls at the famed Cotton Club in Harlem, where the best jazz was being performed by such musical geniuses as Duke Ellington and Cab Calloway. Ruby thought the opportunity couldn't be missed. Never mind that the girls would have to skip half the school year.

Now 14 years old, Dorothy Dandridge met some of the nation's best black entertainers at the Cotton Club. Among them was Harold Nicholas, half of the Nicholas Brothers dance team. Thus began a four-year courtship, which was mostly carried on at long distance as both pursued their careers.

The Dandridge Sisters toured Europe in 1939, but returned home early when World War II broke out. Soon they were back at the Cotton Club, once again on stage with Bill "Bojangles" Robinson.

In 1940 Dandridge, now 18 years old, won her first leading role in a movie entitled *Four Shall Die*, which would later be renamed *The Condemned Men*. Hollywood made much of producing this all-black motion picture, which was supposed to make a breakthrough in the race relations department—meaning that white viewers would want to see it, too—but the outcome was pretty much of a disaster. Theaters just wouldn't take the film.

Though beautiful and talented, Dorothy Dandridge spent much of her career toiling in obscure films. The reason: race.

Soon after, Dandridge got a part in a John Wayne movie called *Lady from Louisiana*, but she really became noticed when famed Fox Studio production head Darryl F. Zanuck cast her as a singer in a musical called *Sun Valley Serenade* with ice skating star Sonja Henie and the great bandleader Glenn Miller. Dandridge's key scene occurs when she appears with the band in a satiny dress, walks past the onstage Nicholas Brothers, and sings this question, "Pardon me, boy, is that the Chattanooga Choo Choo?" It was a hit.

Her career continued to roll, most notably with *Jump for Joy*, the Ellington musical that was to challenge Hollywood racial stereotypes. But Harold Nicholas had different ideas and wanted to marry Dandridge, who at age 18 had grown into a stunningly beautiful woman.

In September 1942, they were married and Dandridge hoped to settle down to a more or less fairy-tale domestic life. But the marriage went downhill from the start. Dandridge soon found that her husband was constantly unfaithful. In 1943 she gave birth to their daughter, Harolyn—called Lynn—but complications followed. By the time Lynn was three years old, it was evident that the child was mentally disabled. Dandridge would raise her daughter as her mother had raised her and her sister—alone. She and Harold were divorced in 1950, but not before the heartbreak of her daughter's condition and her loveless marriage had taken its toll. She sank into a deep depression and tried to commit suicide twice in 1948 with overdoses of sleeping pills.

Despite her many problems, Dandridge managed to pull herself together, and she embarked on a second career as an actress and singer. First, she studied for two years at the Actors' Laboratory in Los Angeles. Then, concentrating on elegant torch songs from such composers as Cole Porter and clad in stunning

Dandridge and John Justin in a scene from Island in the Sun. *The 1957 movie broke new ground for Hollywood, depicting interracial romance.*

gowns, she became immensely popular and financially secure by singing at glamorous nightclubs around the country.

Audiences, black and white alike, regarded Dandridge as a beautiful woman. But according to the social customs and beliefs of the times, it was unthinkable that she should have any kind of romantic interest—on- or offscreen—with a white man. In fact, it was not until the 1957 release of a movie called *Island in the Sun* that Hollywood first filmed a black woman in the arms of a white man. Set in the West Indies, the movie concerned politics and interracial romance. It starred James

Mason and Joan Fontaine, with Dandridge getting third billing.

The dilemma over filming the romantic scenes in this movie is interesting, particularly since the plot revolved around two interracial romances, very daring for this time. Dandridge assumed the role of Margot Seaton, a woman of the islands who has a love affair with a white newspaperman, played by John Justin. Harry Belafonte, playing a union organizer, would become involved with a wealthy white woman on the islands, played by Joan Fontaine. The studio decided that their "romance" could go no further than a longing glance. But the relationship between a black woman—Dandridge—and a white man—Justin— would be allowed to blossom into love, and they would even be allowed to go to England together. And in addition to all this, there was a third romance in this rather strange-for-the-times movie. The daughter of a powerful white island family, played by Joan Collins, has an affair with the governor's son and is about to bear a child. The movie implies that the reason for this "sin" is because she is mistakenly led to believe that she has "black blood," a discovery that implies she would be led to "immoral" acts. After much teeth gnashing, the studio decided on the ground rules for the interracial relationships in the film: no kissing between the races and no on-screen marriages.

In the meantime, Dandridge was concerned about the unrealistic portrayals in the film. Here were two people supposed to be hopelessly in love and the script wouldn't even let them admit it out loud, let alone kiss! The more the production staff ignored her complaints, the angrier and more uncooperative she became.

Finally, the studio relented—a little. Dandridge and Justin still couldn't kiss, but at least he could say, "You know I'm in love with you, don't you?"

instead of "You know how I feel." Then it was decided that the romantic scenes would be filmed in two versions. One would be "sanitized" for American audiences, and the other, for Europeans, would be a little more realistic.

Even with all the concessions, the reactions against *Island in the Sun* were strong, most especially in the South. Memphis, Tennessee, banned the film entirely. Drive-in theaters in Alabama and North Carolina were threatened with violence if they showed it. The South Carolina legislature even considered passing a bill that would fine any theater that showed it $5,000.

Despite all that, the film made a profit of about $8 million, a considerable sum at that time. It seemed to prove that in most areas of the country, the general audience could survive very nicely with interracial romance.

But this constant undercurrent of controversy, as well as reversals in her career and personal life, took a toll on Dandridge. She often soothed her frustrations with tranquilizers, alcohol, and sleeping pills. In 1959, she married white nightclub owner Jack Denison. Many thought the interracial marriage would harm her career; instead, it simply harmed her. The relationship turned abusive, and they were divorced. She later said that Denison had married her to gain money for his financially troubled businesses. Indeed, at the time of their divorce in 1959, she was forced to pay off his enormous debts as part of the divorce settlement. That brought her to near financial ruin for a time. No longer able to afford special care for Lynn, now a teenager, Dandridge was forced to put her only child in an institution. Dandridge did gain some film notice with performances in movies such as *Tarzan's Peril* (1951) and *Bright Road* (1953), in which she played a schoolteacher opposite school principal Harry Belafonte. For once she was not cast as a sex symbol, and she proved her ability to act.

Dandridge enjoys a laugh with her costars, Harry Belafonte (left) and Robert Mitchum, during the filming of Carmen Jones. *Director Otto Preminger is at right.*

But the height of Dandridge's film career occurred in 1954 when she was cast as the lead in *Carmen Jones*, an all-black version of Georges Bizet's opera *Carmen*. Her performance was extraordinary and earned her an Oscar nomination, marking the first time a black actress had ever been nominated in the Best Actress category. She was also the first black woman ever to appear on the cover of *Life* magazine. It looked as though an exciting new career was before her. *Time* magazine called her "one of the outstanding dramatic actresses of the screen."

Following the filming, Dandridge began an affair with the director, the famed Otto Preminger. For years, their romance remained a great open secret in Hollywood. It was said that she hoped they would marry, but some years later he left her. In 1959, Dandridge won a Golden Globe award for her portrayal of Bess in George Gershwin's *Porgy and Bess*.

Dorothy Dandridge and Harry Belafonte in a tense scene from Otto Preminger's Carmen Jones.

Perhaps now, she thought, the doors would open. But the old racial barriers were as high and strong as before, and she appeared in a series of mediocre films. In *The Decks Ran Red* (1958), she played the only woman on board a mutinous ship. In *Tamango* (1959), she was aboard a slave ship bound for Cuba. In *Malaga* (1962), a tale of robbery, Dandridge's skin color was said to be "immaterial." Hollywood didn't seem to know what else to do with Dandridge.

Troubled in her personal life, thwarted in her acting career, Dandridge relied more and more on alcohol and pills. Then, as though making one last attempt to pull her life together, she signed a contract for two movies in 1965 and a singing engagement for two weeks in New York City. But those films were never made and she never sang again.

Dorothy Dandridge died in her Los Angeles apartment on September 8, 1965, from an overdose of an antidepressant drug. Did she actually intend to kill herself? No one knows for sure. She had tried it before, she abused drugs and alcohol, and she was often despondent.

Almost 30 years later, Halle Berry felt a compelling need to bring to life this tragic story that in many ways paralleled her own life. She was also determined to play the role. "I had never seen a black woman quite like that in a film. She was someone I could admire and aspire to be like," says Halle.

Halle herself spent six years in helping to bring this story to the television screen. She faced rejection after rejection from the Hollywood establishment,

Halle as Dorothy Dandridge and Klaus Maria Brandauer as Otto Preminger in a scene from Introducing Dorothy Dandridge.

Halle as Dandridge in front of a poster for Carmen Jones *in a scene from* Introducing Dorothy Dandridge.

which did not think the plight of Dorothy Dandridge would interest its audience. After beating out actresses Whitney Houston, Janet Jackson, and Vanessa L. Williams for the title role but still getting nowhere, she finally decided to assume the responsibilities of coexecutive producer of the project, which would be filmed for HBO television. This meant that she could be in control of all parts of the production. She was determined to make the story as authentic as

Dandridge and Sidney Poitier in Porgy and Bess.

possible. Many of the dance sequences, for instance, were shot on the same sites where Dandridge performed. Elaborate scenes were duplicated from *Sun Valley Serenade, Carmen Jones,* and *Porgy and Bess.* More than 80 costumes were designed for Halle alone. Halle also sought to present an accurate picture of the intense racial bigotry of the period. In a memorable scene at a Las Vegas hotel, Dandridge discovers that the pool is for whites only. Defiantly, she

Halle Berry kisses Martha Coolidge, the director of Introducing Dorothy Dandridge, *at a film festival in France.*

puts her toe in the water and leaves. When she returns, she discovers that the entire pool has been drained and cleaned. These are not pretty scenes, but Halle, far more than other actresses who might have gotten the role, could understand them, and could relate intensely to the role of Dorothy Dandridge. She said, "I thought this was something I would love to do as an actress. But I also thought Dorothy never got the due she deserved in her lifetime. Someone needed to finally give her that recognition."

Dorothy Dandridge fought a losing battle to be recognized for herself. Halle Berry proved that her battle could be won.

7

ALL THIS AND LOVE TOO

Halle Berry and her husband, Eric Benet, arrive at the 2000 Golden Globe Awards. The two currently live in Los Angeles with Benet's daughter, India.

CHILDHOOD PROBLEMS, a diagnosis of diabetes, a series of abusive or ill-fated romantic entanglements, a failed marriage—is there life for Halle Berry after all this? For a while, Halle wasn't so sure. She said she once got so depressed that she thought of taking her own life. She went so far as to go to the garage and sit in the car, then she just cried for hours, thinking she couldn't face things anymore. "I think that's the weakest I have ever been in my life," she says today. Most of all, it was the breakup of her marriage that made her so despondent. "It took away my self-esteem," she recalls. "It beat me down to the lowest of the lows."

Fortunately, Halle had an inner strength to call on during those terribly trying times. She learned the valuable lesson that she should not depend on a man—neither husband nor boyfriend nor father—for her own self-esteem and place in life. She began to realize that she could depend upon herself to feel worthwhile, a powerful inner lesson that took away her depression and prevented tragedy. Says Halle, "Today I wouldn't even think of sitting in a garage with the car motor on."

However, Halle does admit to relying on her two beloved dogs, Petey and Bumper. "They give unconditional love," she says. And, of course, throughout her life, she has always known that her mother was

Clockwise from top left: Diahann Carroll, Cicely Tyson, and Whoopi Goldberg, actresses Halle Berry identifies as "women who have helped me to define myself."

behind her. During a dark period of her daughter's life, Judith Berry packed a bag, took some time off from her work in Cleveland, and headed west. She held her daughter's hand, listened to her sorrow, and gave her comfort and straight talk.

Since there was nowhere to go but up, Halle set about doing that. She went into therapy, bent on ridding herself of her dependency on her former husband. Although the therapy was helpful, her best medicine was work. Making this her main concentration, she began to look more critically at roles that were offered, with an eye toward searching for parts that were not necessarily meant for a black actress. "Now is the time to get away from racial themes," she said. "Everyone deals with prejudice. But it's time to move on."

In 1996, she refused to join a protest organized by the Reverend Jesse Jackson outside the Oscar ceremonies. Jackson was decrying the small number of black performers nominated each year. Halle's position was that it is important to maintain a positive attitude. "It's easy to get negative about the lack of African Americans nominated," she said, "but there's good stuff going on too."

Halle Berry doesn't cast herself as a role model for young people, but she acknowledges Diahann Carroll, Cicely Tyson, and Whoopi Goldberg as the "women who helped me to define myself." As a high-profile woman in the black community, Halle does hope that she will eventually be able to serve as a role model. "Maybe I'll never get there," she says, "but that's what will keep me going."

Others have already begun to recognize her contributions. In 1997, the Harvard Foundation, an organization that fosters race relations at Harvard University, honored Halle as Cultural Artist of the Year. The honor cites her achievements as an actress, her contributions to race relations in the performing arts, and her community service to all people of

In 1997 Halle won an award at the 3rd Annual Blockbuster Awards.

color. In addition, the National Organization for the Advancement of Colored People (NAACP) gave her its entertainer of the year award for 1999.

Halle sports a new image on the outside as well as the inside these days. Her long gorgeous hair is now short and simple. "The simpler the better," she says. "For the most part I keep my beauty regimen pretty basic." Her clothes are chic and sleek. In fact, her new look so impressed Revlon cosmetics that she was chosen as a spokesperson.

In addition to her film and television work, Halle is also a Revlon spokeswoman. She's seen here in a Revlon 1998 Run/Walk for Women T-shirt.

In the health department also, Halle believes in the basics: sleep and proper nutrition. She hopes eventually to control her diabetes with diet alone.

And how about a new romance? In December 1999, Halle announced that she and singer Eric Benet were engaged. He was present at the Cleveland premiere of *Introducing Dorothy Dandridge* and had proposed to her in her hometown. Benet, a contemporary gospel singer with urban soul and hip-hop influences, was born in Milwaukee, Wisconsin, in

A smiling Halle poses for photographers after receiving the 1999 NAACP award for entertainer of the year.

1970. He has been in the music business since he was a teenager, in a vocal group called Benet, which also included his sister and a cousin. Benet has recieved critical acclaim for his recordings *True to Myself* and *A Day in the Life*.

Halle made it into the headlines again in January 2000, but it wasn't to accept an award. She was driving home alone in a rented sport utility vehicle when she ran a red light and hit a compact car driven by Hetal Raythatha. Halle recieved a gash to her forehead that required about 20 stitches to close.

Raythatha broke her wrist and received bumps and bruises in the collision. She was pulled from the wreckage when firefighters arrived at the scene. Halle was nowhere to be found. It was later reported that she had driven home in a daze after the collision and that her fiancé Benet had taken her to Cedars-Sinai Medical Center for treatment of the cut to her forehead. Halle would give many versions of the accident to the authorities and to the press, but they all amounted to the same story—she drove home alone, crashed into something with her car, awoke in a daze, saw no other damaged vehicles, realized her forehead was bleeding, and drove home for treatment.

Halle and Eric Benet share a tender moment backstage at the 2000 Emmy Awards.

Garnering awards for her performance in Introducing Dorothy Dandridge. *This page: the Golden Globe. Opposite page: the Emmy.*

She filed a police report, but reporters and Raythatha accused her of leaving the scene of an accident. Lurid tales of a hit-and-run accident appeared in the tabloid press, and Raythatha sued Berry, claiming that she had been disabled as a result of the accident. The tales in the press caused many to wonder who was telling the truth concerning the incident. Halle pleaded no contest to leaving the scene of an accident, a misdemeanor. She was fined $13,500, placed on three years' probation, and ordered to put in 200 hours of community service. Some critics said this was just a typical slap on the wrist because the defendant was an actress. Jodi Brandt, a deputy district attorney, denied that Halle Berry was given preferential treatment. "The offer we gave is the offer we give any other woman that walks through this door," Brandt said. As of early 2001, Raythatha's lawsuit against Halle was still pending. The actress settled an earlier lawsuit over an automobile collision out of court for an undisclosed amount of money.

Like Berry, Eric has had to overcome some sorrow of his own. Several years ago, the mother of his daughter, India, was killed in a car crash.

When she accepted her Golden Globe award for *Introducing Dorothy Dandridge,* a confident, self-assured Halle Berry spoke to the audience. She acknowledged that her mother had told her to enjoy this moment. "Well, Mom . . . I'm enjoying it!" she said. She also spoke to Eric, her fiancé, saying, "You have given me the biggest gift anybody can give me and that is the freedom to be who I am and for loving me anyway." And she spoke about Dorothy Dandridge. "Tonight as you honor me, whom you really honor is the eminent Dorothy Dandridge. She never got to stand here and be recognized by her peers, but because she lived, I am able to. Thank you so much."

Following her Golden Globe award, Halle found that she had been nominated for an Emmy for the same role. The Emmy Awards show is television's big night to celebrate the best performances of the past year. As the show progressed, Martin Sheen and Rob Lowe took the stage to announce the winner for Best Actress in a Mini-Series or Made for Television Movie. The envelope was opened, and Halle Berry had won another award for her performance as Dorothy Dandridge. She took the stage, and upon receiving her Emmy Award, said, "Wherever Dorothy Dandridge is right now, she is standing tall and proud. Thank you to my community, the African-American community, who picks me up when I'm down and never, ever lets me go." *Introducing Dorothy Dandridge* would go on to win a total of six Emmy Awards that year.

Receiving awards for her performances was certainly one of the high points of the year 2000 for Halle. But there was still more to come. In June, the film *The X-men* opened in theaters. The film, based on a Marvel comic book, told the story of a band of superheroes who try to stop a villain from attacking a conference of world leaders in New York City. One of those superheroes was Ororo Monroe, known as Storm. Storm, able to control weather such as rain and lightning, was played by Halle with a long, flowing, white wig and special contact lenses. The role was a difficult one. Halle had to perform many physically demanding scenes, including fights with the film's villains and flying through the air. When the film was completed and finally appeared in theaters, it was a huge success. At the end of the year, *The X-men* was one of the top 10-highest-grossing films for the year 2000, taking in over $157 million.

In 2001 Halle appeared in *Swordfish*, a crime-thriller about hackers trying to steal money from the government. The film costars John Travolta

and Hugh Jackman, who played Wolverine alongside Halle in *X-men*. Halle will also continue to work with Jackman as 20th Century Fox has announced plans for a sequel to *The X-men*, which is expected to begin filming later in the year 2001.

Halle Berry's life took an exciting turn in January of 2001. She married Eric Benet in a secret ceremony described as "exotic" by her representative Vincent Spade. It would seem that Halle is ready to move into a new era of happiness. As usual in Hollywood, the tabloid press is already predicting a breakup of her marriage. Berry and Benet have sued the *Star* for $5 million for libel over remarks that their marriage is "on the rocks."

Halle Berry's life has often appeared to mirror that of Dorothy Dandridge, but there is one major difference. Halle has struggled, challenged the Hollywood system, and succeeded. Dorothy Dandridge fought the odds and lost too early. But just the fact

In The X-men, one of the most successful films of 2000, Halle played the role of Storm, a superhero who can control the weather.

that she was there made it a little easier for Halle Berry. In her acceptance speech for her Best Actress Oscar in 2002, Halle thanked many of the black actresses that paved the way for her success. And Halle vows that her own work will make it easier still for the next generation of young people with talent, courage, and many long hills to climb.

CHRONOLOGY

———— ❧ ————

1968   Halle Berry born in Cleveland, Ohio, August 1

1972   Father leaves household; family later moves to Bedford Hills, Ohio

1986   Wins Miss Teen Ohio beauty pageant; graduates from Bedford High; enters Cuyahoga College but leaves for Chicago after less than a year

1989   Moves to New York City; wins part in short-lived TV series *Living Dolls*; diagnosed with diabetes

1991   Appears in movies *Jungle Fever*, *The Last Boy Scout*, and *Strictly Business*

1992   Appears in movie *Boomerang*, TV miniseries *Queen*; meets baseball player David Justice; named one of the world's most beautiful people by *Us* and *People* magazines

1993   Marries Justice on January 1; appears in *The Program* and *The Flintstones*

1995   Appears in *Solomon and Sheba* and *Losing Isaiah*

1996   Appears in *Executive Decision*, *The Rich Man's Wife*, and *Race the Sun*; divorces Justice

1998   Appears in *Why Do Fools Fall in Love?*, *The Wedding*, and *Bulworth*

1999   Stars in TV movie *Introducing Dorothy Dandridge*; wins NAACP's Entertainer of the Year Award; announces engagement to Eric Benet in December; wins Golden Globe award for Best Actress in a Mini-series or TV Movie for her role in *Introducing Dorothy Dandridge*

2000   Involved in automobile accident, fined $13,500 and sentenced to three years of probation and 200 hours of community service

2001   Marries Eric Benet in secret ceremony in January; she and Benet sue the *Star* for $5 million for libel over remarks the marriage is "on the rocks"

2002   Becomes first African American to win an Oscar for Best Actress for her role in *Monster's Ball*; wins the Screen Actor's Guild award in the actress category for *Monster's Ball*

FILMOGRAPHY

———— ❦ ————

Films

Jungle Fever

The Last Boy Scout

Strictly Business

The Program

The Flintstones

Solomon and Sheeba

Losing Isaiah

Executive Decision

The Rich Man's Wife

Race the Sun

B.A.P.S

Why Do Fools Fall in Love?

Bulworth

The X-men

Pluto Nash

Swordfish

Monster's Ball

Television

Living Dolls

Knots Landing

Queen

Introducing Dorothy Dandridge

The Wedding

FURTHER READING

Blankenhorn, David. *Fatherless in America*. New York: Basic Books, 1995.

Blue, Rose, and Corinne J. Naden. *Staying Out of Trouble in a Troubled Family*. Brookfield, Conn.: Millbrook, 1998.

Boyle, Donald. *Dorothy Dandridge*. New York: St. Martin's Press, 1997.

Gay, Kathlyn. *The Rainbow Effect: Interracial Families*. New York: Franklin Watts, 1987.

Isaacs, Annasuya. "Halle Berry, Phoenix Rising." *City & Suburban Styles*, Summer/Fall 1999.

Juliana, Joseph, M.D. *When Diabetes Complicates Your Life*. Minneapolis, Minn.: Chronimed, 1993.

Layden, Joe. *Domestic Violence*. Brookfield, Conn.: Millbrook, 1994.

Webb, Michael. *Happy Birthday, Hollywood: One Hundred Years of Magic, 1887–1987*. Hollywood, Calif.: Motion Picture and Television Fund, 1987.

"You Sure Don't Fit the Profile." *Newsweek*, January 1, 2000.

INDEX

———— ❦ ————

PICTURE CREDITS

ROSE BLUE, an author and educator, has written more than 50 books, both fiction and nonfiction, for young readers. Her books have appeared as TV specials and have won many awards. A native New Yorker, she lives in the borough of Brooklyn.

CORINNE NADEN, a former U.S. Navy journalist and children's book editor, also has more than 50 books to her credit. A freelance writer, she lives in Tarrytown, New York, where she shares living quarters with her two cats, Tigger and Tally Ho!